GREAT SPIRIT

North American Indian Portraits

PHONE NO. 3

GREAT SPIRIT

North American Indian Portraits

COMPILED BY

Edward McAndrews

CARL MAUTZ PUBLISHING

EDWARD MCANDREWS

NEVADA CITY 1998

First Edition
COPYRIGHT 1998
ALL RIGHTS RESERVED IN ALL COUNTRIES
CARL MAUTZ PUBLISHING & EDWARD MCANDREWS

EDITED BY ROSEMARIE MOSSINGER
DESIGNED BY RICHARD D. MOORE
COMPOSED IN MONOTYPE BASKERVILLE TYPES
PRINTED BY THOMSON-SHORE INC. IN THE U.S.A.

LIBRARY OF CONGRESS CATALOG CARD NUMBER: 97-069968
CATALOGING-IN-PUBLICATION DATA
McAndrews, Edward.
   Great Spirit: North American Indian portraits / Edward McAndrews.
   —1st ed.
   p. cm.
   Includes bibliographical references and index.
   ISBN: 1-887694-10-2

   1. Indians of North America—Portraits. 2. Indians of North America—Photographs.
3. Photographers—United States. I. Title.

E89.M33 1998   779'.2
               QBI97-41063

FRONTISPIECE: YELLOW SHIRT, ROSEBUD SIOUX
CHARLES HENRY CARPENTER, SILVER PRINT, 1904

CARL MAUTZ PUBLISHING
228 COMMERCIAL STREET, NO. 522
NEVADA CITY, CALIFORNIA 95959
TELEPHONE 916 478-1610 FAX 916 478-0466

This book is dedicated to the Native Americans
who perished at Wounded Knee in the winter of 1889-90
and, with much love, to my mother.

ACKNOWLEDGMENTS

I am grateful to those who gave generously of their time and help. Special thanks to Tom Bell, Fremont archivist; Dr. James S. Brust, collector, author; Richard Buchen, historian, Southwest Museum; Michael Cirelli, collector; Mike Cowdrey, historian, professor; Jan Duggan, teacher, entrepreneur; Patricia Fitzgerald, granddaughter of Reverend Petzelot; Skip Gentry, collector; Emmanuel Gutierrez, administration design; Roderick Ironside, grandson of J. A. Boston; Jerry Kearn, retired Library of Congress archivist; Belvadine Lecher, Dawes County Historical Society; Lora Jean Louthow, related to J. V. Dedrick; Brent Maddox, Getty Research Department; Augie D. Mastroguiseppe, Denver Public Library; Carl Mautz, collector, author, attorney; Jeanne M. Mizener, great-granddaughter of Louis Monaco; Bill Morris, son of Charles Morris; Graham Nash, collector, musician; Arthur L. Olivas, Museum of New Mexico Archives; Dick Punnett, historian; Richard Russelli, author, Museum of New Mexico historian, collector, researcher; Mary Lou Williams, related to William Martin, photographer; and Rosemary Zetter, related to Barthelmess' granddaughter.

Many thanks to Sue Abbey, Sharlot Hall Museum, Arizona; Tracy Baker, James Jerome Hill Reference Library, Arizona; Tracy Baker, Minnesota Historical Society; Deborah Anna Baroff, Museum of the Great Plains, Oklahoma; Kathleen Baxter, National Museum of American History, Smithsonian Institute; Mary Bell, Buffalo & Erie County Historical Society; Diane Brenner, Municipality of Anchorage, Alaska; Nicolette Bromberg, University of Kansas; Richard Bucher, Southwest Museum, California; Paul Camps, University of South Florida; John Carter, Nebraska State Historical Society; Mary Davis, Pike's Peak Library District, Colorado; Roderick Dew, Colorado Springs Fine Arts Center; Richard Engman, University of Washington; Lora Feucht, Nez Perce County Historical Society Inc.; L. Fisk, San Diego Museum of Man, California; Paula Fleming, Smithsonian Anthropological Archives; George Gilbert, American Photographic Historical Society, Inc., New York; B. Gill, Octavia Fellini Public Library, New Mexico; George Grant, Metropolitan Toronto Reference Library, Canada; Fairbanks Hales, University of Alaska; John Hanes, University of Wyoming; Dale Johnson, University of Montana; Jerry Kern, Library of Congress, Washington, D.C.; Harold Lee and Billy Plumbett, Brigham Public Library, Utah; Rebecca Lintz, Colorado Historical Society; Ally Lord, University of Arkansas; Janice Mahew, George Eastman House, New York; Weston Naef, John Paul Getty Museum; Joan Nitzel, Canadian County Genealogical Society; Richard Pearce-Moses, Arizona State Museum; Peter Palmquist, The Daguerreian Society; Helen Plummer, Amon Carter Museum, Texas; Peter Robertson, National Archives of Canada; Susan Seyl, Oregon Historical Society; Joan Singleton, Blockwell Public Library, Oklahoma; Rod Slemmons, Seattle Art Museum; Todd Strand, State Historical Society of North Dakota; J. Sutherland, Northern Arizona University; J. D. Thiesen, Bethel College Mennonite Library and Archives, Kansas; Sharon Uhler, Colorado Springs Pioneer Museums; L. Vaughan, Wyoming State Museum; Lynette Walton, Glenbow Museum, Canada; and Patsy West, Historical Society of South Florida; Robert Lewis, attorney and collector.

Thanks to the staff of the Arizona State University; Boston Public Library; British Museum; Bureau of Vital Statistics, Wyoming; California State Board of Health; California State Bureau of Vital Statistics; California State University, Northridge; Carson City Library, Nevada; Cherokee Strip Land Museum; Chicago Historical Society; Chicago Public Library; City of Pasadena; Cumberland County Historical Society, Pennsylvania; Daytona Beach Community College, Florida; Dodge County Historical Society, Nebraska; El Paso Public Library, Texas; Field Museum of Natural History, Illinois; Florida Department of State Division of Historical Resources; Fort Sheridan Post Library, Illinois; Fremont County Pioneer Museum, Wyoming; Huntington Free Library Reading Room, New York; Idaho State Historical Society; Jacksonville Public Libraries; Kansas State Historical Society; Klamath County Museum, Oregon; Lake County Museum, Illinois; Lawton Public Library, Oklahoma; Lewis & Clark State College; Lewiston City Library, Idaho; Metropolitan Library System; Milwaukee Public Museum, Wisconsin; Missouri Historical Society; Mitchell Indian Museum, Kendall College, Illinois; Mojave County Historical Society, Arizona; Montana Historical Society; Museum of Fair Trade, Nebraska; Museum of New Mexico; Nakoda Museum; Nevada Historical Society; New York Public Library; Newberry Library, Illinois; Oklahoma State University; Omaha Public Library; Pasadena Historical Society, California; St. Lucie County Historical Museum; Seminole Miccosukee Photo Archives; Seminole Tribe of Florida Education Division; Silverton Public Museum, Colorado; Southwest Oklahoma Genealogical Society; Southwest Regional Library, Durango, Colorado; United States Department of the Interior, Yosemite National Park Service, California; University of Oregon; University of Texas at El Paso; Utah State Historical Society; Washington State Historical Society in Tacoma; Wauboneee Comunity College, Illinois; Whyte Museum of the Canadian Rockies; Wyoming State Vital Statistics; and Yellowstone Association.

CONTENTS

Introduction ix

Plates i

Biographies 81

Bibliography 89

Index 91

Unidentified Crow men
Richard Throssel, silver print, c. 1908

I am pleased to present these vintage images of American Indians from my twenty-five-year collection. I hope it will inspire others to bring to light photographs that lie hidden in archives and private collections. Most of the biographical information was gathered from old newspapers, texts, letters, articles from the public archives, directories, public agencies, and private collections. It was a joy to research these photographers, and an honor to meet and talk with some of their great-grandchildren and other descendants.

The photographers who captured these images were often as versatile and colorful as the people they photographed. They ranged from professionals who took hundreds of photographs during their careers, to amateurs and entrepreneurs, such as artists, musicians, journalists, mayors, soldiers, cattle ranchers, a justice of the peace, doctor, U.S. commissioner, and even a state senator. They traveled America by army mule, bicycle, boat, early automobile, and by railroad car, outfitted with complete photo studios. Some worked as government surveyors, others for the railroads, and still others owned or worked in galleries that specialized in portraits of Indians, babies, landscapes, reality and romanticism. The photographers' wives or other women of the household played important roles, assisting in the studio while the men took long photography jaunts. In many cases, they learned the trade, operated the darkroom, and many wives continued to run the business after their husbands died.

These photographs have been used in numerous ways, from advertising tobacco to promoting state tourism. The images of some famous chiefs were reproduced by engravers for U.S. currency, coins, and postage stamps. Some of the poses and settings may seem contrived to the modern eye, but they still powerfully convey the dignity, strength and pride of the Indian people.

Comanche family
George Anthony Addison, cabinet card, c. 1900

Aunk Ah-Mo, Comanche
George Anthony Addison, cabinet card, c. 1900

Unidentified Northern Cheyenne from Buffalo Bill's Wild West Show
Abraham Bogardus, cabinet card

White Swan
Roland Bonaparte, large format albumen print

Yuma Warriors, Lamanda Park, California
Elia A. Bonine

Maria, Flathead
Edward Hugo Boos, silver print, c. 1907

Dick Charlie, wife and child, Ute
Jacob Adam Boston, cabinet card, 1892

Havarcho's daughter, Ute
Jacob Adam Boston, cabinet card, 1890

Mother and child, Blackfoot
Henry Bird Calfee, cabinet card, 1888

Geronimo, Chiricahua Apache
Charles Henry Carpenter, silver print, 1904

Ouray's right-hand men; Wa-rets, at left, and Shavano with pistol.
William Gunnison Chamberlain, cabinet card, 1882

Ouray, Head Chief of the Utes
William Gunnison Chamberlain

Calletano and Jake, Navajo
Dana B. Chase, cabinet card

Pueblo girl, Pajuaque, Santa Clara Pueblo
Dana B. Chase, cabinet card

Southern Utes
James H. Crockwell, cabinet card, albumen print, c. 1885

Black Tongue, Cheyenne
William Richard Cross, carte-de-visite, 1878

No. 395 Spotted Tail's Girl.

Spotted Tail's daughter, Sioux
William Richard Cross, cabinet card

Makah basket weavers
Asahel Curtis, photo postcard

Eskimo mother and children
Beverly Dobbs, silver print

Little Mikinas, Nome, Alaska
Beverly Dobbs, silver print

Cheyenne
Jeremiah B. Drake, imperial cabinet card

Cho-sha-wat-sah, God Man, Osage
Oscar Drum, cabinet card, c. 1908

Red Cloud, Oglala Sioux
Charles Leon Eason, silver print, 1905

Chief Little Wound, Oglala Sioux
Charles Leon Eason, silver print, 1905

Wolf Voice and Friend, Gros Ventre
John Hale Fouch, stereoview, c. 1870

Madonna, *Cayuse*
Benjamin A. Gifford, cabinet card, c. 1905

Dug-Toi-Vigoi, Prairie Chief, Southern Cheyenne
Delancey W. Gill, silver print

Chief Joseph, Nez Perce
Delancey W. Gill, silver print

Chief Iron Tail
Frank Whitman Glasier, silver print

New Haired Horse, wife and child of Stampede, Sioux
Ray W. Graves, cabinet card, c. 1900

Alligator Joe, Tommy Jumper and friends, Seminole
John Frederick Hand, cabinet card

Mother and children, Nez Perce
John Ankar Hanson, cabinet card

Maricopa in Native Costume
Francis A. Hartwell, cabinet card, c. 1889

Maricopa
Francis A. Hartwell, cabinet card, c. 1889

Painted Horse, Sioux
Heyn Brothers, cabinet card, c. 1900

Chief Buckskin Charlie and tribe, Ute
William Edward Hook, imperial cabinet card

Unidentified Navajo weaver
George Wharton James, silver print

Moki snake dancers. Oraibi, imperial albumen print, 1896
George Wharton James, silver print

Unidentified mother and child
Edwin Young Judd, silver print

The Red Man
Gertrude Kasebier, photogravure from *Camera Work*, January, 1903

Chica-Ma-Poo, mother of Yellow Wolf
Edward Latham, silver print, c. 1903

Phoebe Wilpatin in head dress, Nez Perce
Edward Latham, silver print, c. 1903

Chief Brave Heart, Sioux
Henry R. Locke, imperial cabinet card, c. 1890

Yakima children
Walter John Lubken, silver print

Gentle Annie, 90 years old, Havasupai
Frederick Hamer Maude, print from original dry plate negative, 1896

Ranchers at Mission
Frederick Hamer Maude, silver print, 1896

Children of Oraibi Pueblo
Frederick Hamer Maude, silver print, 1896

California mission Indians
Frederick Hamer Maude, silver print

Red Cloud
Fred R. Meyer, silver print, 1907

Piute family
Louis Monaco, carte-de-visite, c. 1875

Gos Hutes warriors
Louis Monaco, carte-de-visite, c. 1875

Samuel American Horse, son of American Horse
Clarence G. Morledge, oversized cabinet card

Buckskin Charlie and wife, Towee
Charles A. Nast, imperial cabinet card

Osage dancers
George W. Parsons, cabinet card, c. 1900

Grandmother, Navajo
William Marion Pennington, silver print

he Grand Mother

The Grandmother, Navajo
William Marion Pennington, silver print

Crow Indian Dancers
William Augustus Petzoldt, postcard

Crow woman
William Augustus Petzoldt, silver print

Crow woman, puppy and child
William Augustus Petzoldt, silver print

Hopi
Horace Swartley Poley imperial cabinet card, c. 1899

Unidentified Cheyenne Chief
William Prettyman, cabinet card, 1880

Apache warrior applying face paint
A. Frank Randall, 1880

Geronimo, Chiricahua Apache, taken at the St. Louis World's Fair
William Rau, stereoview, c. 1904

Little Hawk
William Rau, Silver print

Lone Wolf
Benjamin Franklin Ray, cabinet card, 1880

White Skunk, Comanche Chief
David H. Rodoker, cabinet card, c. 1870

Betsy Boston, Makah
Thomas H. Rutter, imperial cabinet card

Pretty Voice
George W. Scott, cabinet card, 1889

Red Tomahawk and Indian police
George W. Scott, cabinet card, 1889

Red Tomahawk
George W. Scott, cabinet card, 1889

Chief Knife
George W. Scott, print from original dry plate negative

George Eagle Nest
Joseph A. Shuck, postcard

Little Bear, Arapahoe Chief
Joseph A. Shuck, albumen print, 1905

Goggle Sisters, Arapahoe
Charles E. Sproul (won first place at the St. Louis World's Fair), silver print, 1904

Mayodgap, Shoshone
Joseph Elam Stimson, silver print, 1900

Arco family, Comanche
Christopher Charles Stotz, cabinet card, 1880

Unidentified child, Southern Cheyenne
Christopher Charles Stotz, cabinet card, c. 1880

Young Cheyenne warrior
Richard Throssel, silver print,

Isleta Pueblo water carriers
Charles B. Waite, silver print, 1896

Mother and child
Lily Edith White, silver print, 1905

GEORGE ANTHONY ADDISON (1853–1937)
Addison was born in Mississippi, and later moved to Oklahoma where he worked in photography. He produced cabinet cards of the Native Americans of Oklahoma at Fort Sill, the Kiowa, Comanche and Arapahoe. He ran a boarding house in 1899, and in 1901 he opened the Addison House. A year later, he moved his G. A. Addison Hotel to 501 East Avenue in Lawton City, a new town near Fort Sill. Within one year, the Addison Hotel became the town's first hospital. Addison later moved to Shamrock, Texas, and died there at age 84.

ABRAHAM BOGARDUS (1822–1908)
Bogardus had a studio in the heart of New York City, at 872 Broadway on the corner of 18th Street. He took publicity shots of the Indians in William Cody's show.

ROLAND BONAPARTE (1858–1924)
Prince Bonaparte was the grandson of Lucien Bonaparte. He took up photography in his late teens or early twenties, and by age twenty-five he had amassed thousands of photographs from his travels in America and around the world. In 1887, he came to the United States and produced a portfolio of American Indian photographs, now in the Smithsonian Institution, Washington, D.C. He later started a foundation bearing his name in the French Academy of Science, which awarded research grants to young scientists.

ELIA A. BONINE (1843–1916)
Bonine was born in Lancaster, Pennsylvania. He was known as a tent photographer and traveled throughout Arizona taking images of the Mohave, Cocopah and Yuma tribes, the Queen Mine and surrounding areas. In his Indian portraits, he used props such as fancy fringed Victorian chairs, typical of many other photographers of the time. After years of traveling, he settled in Lamanda Park, California. Bonine was known for his landscapes of Pasadena, and for his images of Yuma Indians painted with white clay and dressed for battle.

EDWARD HUGO BOOS (1877–1937)
Boos was born in Kentucky, but spent most of his life in Missoula, Montana, as a reporter in the 25th U.S. Infantry Bicycle Corps' Colored Regiment. He later became advertising manager of the Missoula Mercantile Company. He made excellent images of the Flathead Indians of Montana, including Chief Charlot of the Flathead Reservation.

JACOB ADAM BOSTON (1847–1915)
Boston was born in North Carolina and schooled in Ohio where he learned the photography trade. In 1878, he traveled the West, moved to Pueblo, Cañon City, Saguache, Alamosa, and Pagosa Springs, and finally settled in Durango for nine years. Later he went to Crested Butte and Paonia. He filed a desert land claim in Redvale, built a three-bedroom cabin, and engaged in the ranching business until his death. He is credited with making a striking image of Chief Ignacio and many cabinet cards of the Ute Indians and cowboys of Colorado.

Henry Bird Calfee (1848–1912)

Calfee was a native of Arkansas and moved to Montana. He sketched and painted Yellowstone, and prospected and mined while living in Bozeman Territory. Some of his work was used to illustrate a guidebook of Montana. He was a partner with J. B. Catlin, and they produced stereoviews of Glen Mammoth Springs, Old Faithful Geyser in eruption, Fire Hole River, and Beehive Geyser. Calfee was honored with a creek named after him.

Charles Henry Carpenter (1859–1949)

Carpenter was a chief photographer of the Field Museum from 1899 until he retired, December 31, 1947. He traveled the Hopi reservations, and in 1904, photographed at the Louisiana Purchase Exposition in St. Louis, Missouri, where he made images of many Indian tribes and a portrait of Geronimo.

William Gunnison Chamberlain (1815-1910)

Chamberlain was an early Colorado photographer who settled in Denver in the late 1850s. When he traveled through the mountains looking for good scenic views, his wife ran the studio. He took many images of Chief Ouray, who assumed leadership of the Utes at the age of twenty-seven. During the 1870s, Chamberlain produced more photographs than any other artist in the area. He made cartes-de-visite, stereoviews, cabinet cards, and large formatviews. His motto was "A good Picture or No Pay."

Dana B. Chase (1848–1897)

Chase was born in Maine. The family moved to the Southwest where he found a job as an assistant to Camillus Sidney Fly of Arizona and California. Chase later did photography work for the Santa Fe Southern Railway and traveled to the Santa Clara, San Ildefonso and San Juan pueblos. He owned a studio in Trinidad, Colorado from 1880 to 1885, and traveled between Colorado Springs, Denver, and Santa Fe, New Mexico.

James H. Crockwell (1845–1940)

Crockwell was a noted photographer of Nevada and Utah, and also traveled in eleven states. He was an official photographer for the Chicago World Columbian Exposition of 1893.

William Richard Cross (1839–1907)

Cross had a studio in Niobrara, Nebraska and produced many portraits of the Sioux Indians as cartes-de-visite, stereoscopic views and cabinet cards. He photographed the students of the Saint Francis School at the Rosebud Agency, and, in a venture that may have been financed by the firm of Bailey, Dix & Meade, he made a series of Sitting Bull's camp. Cross also made scenic views of the Black Hills, Bald Mountains, Nevada Gulch, and gold mining.

Asahel Curtis (1874–1941)

Curtis is known for his images of mountains, Alaska, and the Yukon. He began his career by working for his brother, Edward, who became famous for his books on the North American Indians. Asahel Curtis later had his own photographic company, and some of his images were used to promote the Northwest.

BEVERLY DOBBS (1867–1937)
Dobbs was born in Missouri. He learned the photography trade in Lincoln, Nebraska, then moved to Bellingham, Washington, where he had a studio for twenty years. He was awarded one of six gold medals given at the Louisiana Purchase Exposition at the St. Louis World's Fair.

JEREMIAH B. DRAKE (1864–1928)
Drake was originally form Bolivar, Missouri. He settled in Oklahoma City in 1889, and opened the first photography studio in Ponca City after the opening of the Cherokee Strip in 1893. He started his business by photographing the cowboys who came to the local bars.

OSCAR DRUM (1861–1936)
Drum was born in Illinois. He moved to Bartlesville, Oklahoma, and opened his studio in 1905, producing cabinet cards and photo postcards of the area and Native Americans. Some of his images were made into litho postcards. At his funeral, one of the pallbearers was Frank Griggs, another local photographer who was his friend and former partner.

CHARLES LEON EASON (1870–1921)
Eason was born in Galesburg, Illinois, and moved to Chadron, Nebraska with his two brothers, Ed and Will. He opened a photographic studio with one of his brothers. Charles died of tuberculosis in 1921, survived by his wife and his children, Charles and Helen.

JOHN HALE FOUCH (1849–1933)
Fouch was the first post photographer at Fort Keogh, and made a series of stereoviews of Yellowstone, two excellent images of Chief Joseph, and one of the earliest images of Curley, Custer's Crow scout. Fouch is also credited with being the first to photograph the Custer battlefield. He later moved to Minnesota and opened a gallery. He retired in Glendale California.

BENJAMIN A. GIFFORD (1859–1938)
Gifford was the first photographer in Portland, Oregon, and made many images of Columbia River, Mount Hood, and Native Americans.

DELANCEY W. GILL (1859–1940)
Gill, a water color artist, produced illustrations for the American Ethnology Department. After learning the trade of photography, he took images of the Indian delegations that came to Washington to discuss treaties. Gill's photograph of Hollow Horn Bear, a Brule Dakota, was used on the fourteen-cent stamp in 1922.

FRANK WHITMAN GLASIER (1866–1950)
Glasier was born in Massachusetts. He later lived in Brockton where he specialized in 8 x 10 inch glass plates. He was the official photographer for the Barnum & Bailey Circus, and also photographed the Ringling, Sparks and Sells circuses. His specialty was photographing the Indians and Wild West shows.

RAY W. GRAVES (1885–1919) and Fay Graves (1887–1944)
Graves and his wife purchased a studio from Isiah R. McIntire in Chadron, Nebraska. They

produced studio images of the Native Americans of Chadron, and photographed ranching, farming, and early twentieth-century Nebraska.

JOHN FREDERICK HAND (1859–1944)

Hand was born in Germany and emigrated to America in 1874. After growing up and working in Chicago, he moved to Florida in 1898, where he met and married his wife, Olive. Fred and Olive operated a studio and advertised portraits and lantern slides.

JOHN ANKAR HANSON (1854–1923)

Hanson was born in Denmark and moved to the East Coast as a youth. He moved to California and became a partner with Erickson. Hanson later moved to Grangeville City, Idaho, and opened the Elite photography store.

FRANCIS A. HARTWELL (1852–1908)

Hartwell assisted photographer Henry Buchman for three years, became a partner, then opened his own studio six years later. His photographs were used to encourage tourism in Arizona, and he took many images of the Maricopa Indians.

HEYN BROTHERS, GEORGE (1856–1892) and HERMAN (1868–1949)

George came to America from Germany, and probably was the first member of his family to settle in this country. After living in Chicago and learning his trade, George moved to Nebraska and opened the Heyn Photo Supply Company. His brother, Herman, was the proprietor of the Lumiere Studio, and took many images of famous celebrities, including William Howard Taft and Buffalo Bill. Herman and his partner, Mr. James Marazen, produced a collection of full-body shots and portraits of Native Americans that was shown at the 1898 Exposition, and the 1904 Exposition in St. Louis.

WILLIAM EDWARD HOOK (1833–1908)

Hook was born in England. He produced photographic landscapes during his travels in Minnesota, Michigan, Montana, New Mexico, Colorado, California, and Canada. Later he settled in Manitou Springs, Colorado, and opened the Wholesale View Company where he sold some of his images to William Jackson. He moved the business to Colorado Springs in 1890.

GEORGE WHARTON JAMES (1858–1923)

James amassed a collection of Indian artifacts over a period of forty years. Some of the baskets, pottery, textiles, tools and weapons were used to illustrate his books. He worked with photographer and publisher Charles Pierce, and was also a partner with a fellow Englishman, photographer Frederick Maude. James photographed the Hopi, Zuni, Navajo, and Walapai.

EDWIN YOUNG JUDD (1861–1942)

Judd was born in Hartford, Connecticut. A graduate of Yale University, he was known for his intricate business transactions. He was involved in the wool trade of Oregon, and became a member of C. Judd & Root Wool. Within a few years, he built and put into operation the Pendleton Woolen Mills, becoming president of the firm. Judd was based in San Francisco, where he looked after his interest in Pendleton, and was a devotee of the arts, photography, and song writing.

GERTRUDE KASEBIER (1852–1934)
Kasebier was born in Iowa. After studying photography, she opened a portrait studio in New York City near 32nd Street in 1897. One of her prints, *The Manager*, brought the highest price ever paid for a photograph at the time. She was a leading portrait photographer of the day, and was known for family and mother-and-child photographs. Her Native American images were taken of the performers at the Buffalo Bill Show when they were in New York. *The Red Man* was taken in 1898.

EDWARD LATHAM (1845–1928)
Latham was a physician for the U.S. Indian Agency and an amateur photographer. He made hundreds of images of Indians, the Spokane and Columbia Rivers, and other landscapes.

HENRY R. LOCKE (1850–1927)
Locke was born in Huntington, Pennsylvania. He moved to the West and settled in Spearfish, South Dakota, then opened a studio in Lead City. He later bought a studio in Deadwood that may have been owned by J. C. H. Grabill, another noted photographer of Deadwood and the Black Hills. Locke traveled to the Crow Reservation in Montana and opened a studio in Cambria, a small coal-producing town in Wyoming.

WALTER JOHN LUBKEN (1882–1960)
Lubken was born in New York City. He was the official photographer of the Arrowrock Dam construction and the Boulder Dam project, and the staff photographer for the Bureau of Reclamation from 1903 to 1910. He traveled and photographed projects in Arizona, New Mexico and California.

FREDERICK HAMER MAUDE (1858–1960)
Maude was originally from England, and came to America to help Wharton James with photography for his book on the Spanish missions. He also made landscapes and images of Indians who lived near the missions. Maude's Indian photographs are considered some of the finest uncontrived portraits of everyday life. After his death at age 102, his photograph collection was donated to the Southwest Museum in Los Angeles.

FRED R. MEYER (1874–1939)
Meyer was a native of Buffalo, New York. In his earlier years, he traveled to the Dakotas, photographing Indians and learning their crafts and customs. He supplied the museums of New York, Philadelphia, and other cities with some of their most beautiful Indian artifacts. When he died, an Indian dirge of farewell was sung by Chief Richard Big Kettle of the Seneca tribe.

LOUIS MONACO (1842–1897)
Luigi Natale Monaco was born in Switzerland and came to America in 1859. He moved to Virginia City, Nevada at age twenty-two, and by the end of that year he moved to Gold Hill. Seven years later he opened his first photography business, and a year later he opened a gallery in Eureka, Nevada. After 24 years in Nevada, he moved his family and photography business to Market Street in San Francisco, where his company is still in existence. His Indian images are rare.

CLARENCE G. MORLEDGE (1869–1948)
Morledge was a photographer by trade and lived for a time at the Pine Ridge Agency. He photographed many buildings, garrisons, Indians in line on rationing day, the Scalp Dance in 1890,

and the Omaha Dancers in 1891. Some of the Indians he photographed were Little Eagle, Black Dog, and She Came Spotted. Approximately forty images are attributed to Morledge, including the image of his son, Samuel American Horse, reproduced in this book. He frequently used as a background a painting of Indian wars, done in the Miniconju (Lakota) style. Morledge is probably best known for his images of the aftermath at Wounded Knee.

Charles A. Nast (1857–1931)
Nast was born in Ohio and later lived in New York, then moved to Denver and had a studio at 1624 Curtis Street. Charles' brother, John E. Nast, helped him for the first few years. Charles specialized in children's photos and was known as "the baby photographer." He also took images of Indians of the Ute tribe, and some of the photographs of Chief Buckskin, a famous Ute Chief, are credited to him.

George W. Parsons (1845–1926)
Parsons was born in Arkansas. He traveled from Kansas to Oklahoma and settled in Pawhuska, a town in the Osage Nation. Parsons took many exceptionally fine images of the Osage tribes and was the earliest known photographer in the Pawhuska area. He married and had two sons.

William Marion Pennington (1874–1940)
Pennington was born in Kentucky. He and his wife opened a picture theatre in New Mexico, and within a few years moved to Durango, Colorado, and opened a studio with a partner. He is known for his portrait images of the Navajos of Arizona in 8 x 10 inch format. He won many medals for his quality work. Pennington later retired in Alhambra, California.

William Augustus Petzoldt (1872–1960)
Petzoldt was born in Rochester, New York, of German descent. He attended the University of Rochester, and in later years became a Baptist minister. After moving to several states, William and his wife settled in Lodge Grass, Montana at the turn of the century. They opened a school to help educate the Crow natives near their homes, thus preventing the government from sending Indian children out of the state for schooling. Petzoldt regularly traded in his old equipment and used the newest cameras available.

Horace Swartley Poley (1864–1949)
Poley was born in Pennsylvania. He moved to Colorado Springs, Colorado, and opened a photo shop on North Tejon Street; later he became a registry clerk for the Colorado Springs Post Office. Poley took several photographs of Buckskin Charlie, many of the Utes and Indians of Arizona. His slide shows, held at the park pavillion near the street car line, drew large crowds.

William Prettyman (1858–1932)
Prettyman was originally from the East and learned photography from I. Bonsall, a Civil War photographer. He later opened his own gallery in Arkansas City, Kansas, and photographed the Indians of the area. William traveled the countryside, photographing domestic scenes, soldiers, cowboys and Indians. Later, George B. Cornish was his protege and partner, managing the studio in his absence. Prettyman moved to Oklahoma at age thirty-six, and opened another studio where he photographed the Indians of the territory and performers in the Pawnee Bill Show. George Cornish also produced Oklahoma Views, an album of photographs by Prettyman and Cornish. Prettyman became mayor of Blackwell, Oklahoma in the early 1900s.

A. Frank Randall (1854–1916)

A native of Massachusetts, Randall was known for his White Mountain Apache photographs. He made a series of photos of Indian leaders in the spring of 1884 while at the San Carlos Reservation. Some of the tribes he photographed were the Chiricahua, Mohave, Yuma, Jicarilla, and Mescalero. Randall is probably best known for his images of Geronimo, the Chiricahua Apache leader.

William Rau (1855–1920)

Rau was born in Philadelphia. He was known as a portrait photographer, but also took many views of the city, ship-building, landscapes, and railroads. He was the official photographer of the Pennsylvania Railroad in 1890. He photographed Geronimo in 1904 at the St. Louis World's Fair where he was an official photographer.

Benjamin Franklin Ray (1858–1932)

Ray was born in Rushville, Indiana, and moved to Nebraska at an early age. He later became a teacher and took up photography as a hobby, then as a trade. He took many photographs of Rushville and the Native Americans of the town and surrounding areas. Jack Red Cloud, son of the famous chief, was one of Ray's noted subjects. Ray was one of the official photographers at the Pan Pacific Exposition in 1901.

David H. Rodoker (1840–1919)

Rodoker was born in Ashland County, Ohio. After traveling the country for several years, he moved to Illinois where he learned the photography trade. He moved to Kansas in 1874, and opened his own photo business. At some point, he teamed up with Christopher C. Stotz to produce Indian images. Known for his fine work—satisfaction guaranteed—he eventually got a position in the government Photography Department. Many of his images were taken at his galleries in Dexter, Cedarville, and at 814 Main Street in Winfield, Kansas.

Thomas H. Rutter (1837–1925)

Rutter was born in England. He was a veterinarian by trade, and served in the Civil War. He was established as a photographer in 1870 in Butte City, Montana, known for his landscapes and portraits. He also took photos for the Union Pacific Railroad. Years later, he moved to Washington and settled in Yakima where he took many images of the Indians of the Northwest.

George W. Scott (1854–1910)

Scott was born in Washington, D.C. After years of schooling, he joined the service and was sent to Dakota. While stationed in Bismarck and Fort Yates, he took many photographs. Big Head, Pretty Voice, Kills the Enemy, Yellow Horn, White Bull (Sioux), Mad Bear, Paul Elk, John Grass, and Red Tomahawk, the head of the Indian police stationed at Fort Yates, were photographed by Scott. He later moved to Lander, Wyoming, where he opened a studio. In 1907 he took images of a Shoshone tea party. Scott left photography and worked in Lander's first weather station. He died of cancer in California, February 11, 1910.

Joseph A. Shuck (1865–1952)

Born in Ohio, Shuck learned photography by working with a German photographer as an apprentice for three years from the age of thirteen. Six years later, Shuck went to work for a studio in Topeka, Kansas, and later moved to Columbus, Nebraska, where he may have opened a studio. In 1903, Shuck opened a photography studio in El Reno, Oklahoma, where he experimented with new methods and formulas. Shuck made images of the Native American around El Reno, especially the Arapahoe. Some of his Native American images were made into souvenir postcards by the William Stolz Stationery Company. With the assistance of his wife, Shuck operated his studio until a few weeks before his death at the age of 87.

CHARLES E. SPROUL (1883–1923)
Sproul was born in Paris, Missouri. He worked at the Conklin Studio in St. Louis, then moved to Lander, Montana and opened a studio in 1913. He won first place at the St. Louis World's Fair for his image of the Goggle sisters, Arapahoe from the Wind River Reservation.

JOSEPH ELAM STIMSON (1870–1952)
Stimson was an artist and painter, but also was one of the best known photographers of Wyoming. He made many images of Yellowstone, cities and towns, and some of the Native Americans of the region. Stimson was the Union Pacific's official photographer, with a studio in Cheyenne.

CHRISTOPHER CHARLES STOTZ (1851–1932)
Stotz was born in Columbia, Pennsylvania. He opened a studio in El Reno, Oklahoma, working from a tent in the early days of the city. Stotz was known for his quality work. He photographed the people of the region, including many members of local Indian Tribes, such as the Kiowa, Arapaho, and Cheyenne. He left Oklahoma at age 75 and retired, possibly because of his health, and spent the remainder of his life in California.

RICHARD THROSSEL (1881–1933)
Throssel was a French Canadian and Cree Indian; an artist, photographer, avid sportsman, and expert rifleman, as well as a family man. He lived eight years with the Crow Indians, photographed many of the Cheyenne, and produced oil paintings of Western subjects. His photographs were popular with tourists, and were produced in all sizes.

CHARLES B. WAITE (1861–1929)
Waite had a studio at 2111 West 1st Street in Los Angeles, California in 1893, and was known as a landscape photographer. He traveled to Arizona and New Mexico while working for the railroads until c. 1898. Waite later settled in Mexico and made many lantern slides depicting life on the railroads and in the cities of Mexico.

LILY EDITH WHITE (1866–1944)
White was born in Salem, Oregon. She was known as an artist and landscape photographer, and was a member of the Oregon Camera Club. White took photographs of the Columbia River Gorge, Memaloose Island, and Castle Rock, and also made images of the Klickatats and Chief Skookum Wallahu. She later moved to Monterey, California, and died at her home on Scenic Drive in Carmel.

Adam, Clark, "C. C. Stotz: Photographer of Indians," *Central States Archaeological Journal*, Vol. 14, No. 4, October 1967.

Andrews, Ralph W., *Curtis' Western Indians*, Bonanza, New York, 1962.

Andrews, Ralph W., *Indians as the Westerners Saw Them*, Superior Publishing Company, Seattle, 1963.

Bastoni, Gernald R., William Herman Rau, *Lehigh Valley Railroad Photographs, 1899*, Valley Graphic Service, Inc., Bethlehem, Pennsylvania, 1989.

Belous, Russell E. and Robert A. Weinstein, Will Soule: Indian Photographer, (1869-74), The Ward Ritchie Press, Los Angeles, 1969.

Berezin, Ronna H., Unknown Photographer of the West: Elias A. Bonine (1843-1916), Pasadena Historical Society, Pasadena, California, 1982.

Brown, Mark H., and Robert A. Felton, The Frontier Years, Holt, 1955.

Brown, Dee, and Martin F. Schmitt, Fighting Indians of the West, Charles Scribner's Sons, New York and London, 1948.

Brust, Dr. James, Greasy Grass, Custer Battlefield Historical Museum Association, Vol. 7, Montana, 1991.

Bush, Alfred and Lee C. Mitchell, The Photograph and the American Indian, Princeton University Press, Princeton, New Jersey, 1994.

Carl Moon, Photographer & Illustrator of the American Southwest, Argonaut Book Shop, Catalogue 83, San Francisco, 1982.

Carter, Kate B., Early Pioneer Photographers, Salt Lake City, 1975.

Casa Grande, Louis B., and Philip Bourns, *Side Trips to Photography of Sumner W. Matteson 1898-1908*, Milwaukee Public Museum and the Science Museum of Minnesota, 1983.

Castle, Henry A., *History of St. Paul and Vicinity, Vol. 3*, Lewis Publishing Company, 1912.

Clark, Galen, *Indians of the Yosemite*, Reflex Publishing Company, Redondo Beach, California, 1910.

Cunningham, Robert E., ed., *Norman, Indian Territory: A Frontier Photographic Record by W. S. Prettyman*, Robert E. Cunningham, ed., University of Oklahoma Press, 1958.

Current, Karen, *Photography and the Old West*, Amon Carter Museum, Fort Worth, Texas, 1978.

Daniel, Peter and Raymond Smock, *A Talent for Detail*, Indian School, Carlyle, Pennsylvania.

Denver City Directory. (c. 1892)

Doten, Alf, unpublished journal.

Driebe, Tom, *In Search of the Wild Indian*, Maurose Publishing Company, Moscow, Pennsylvania, 1997.

Evans, Susan, "Henry Buehman: Tucson Photographer (1874-1912)," *History of Photography*, Vol. 5, No. 1, 1981.

Farr, William E., *The Reservation Blackfeet*, University of Washington Press, Seattle and London, 1984.

Federal Census Records.

Fleming, Paula Richardson and Judith Luskey, *The North American Indians in Early Photographs*, Dorset Press, New York, 1986.

Fly, Mrs. M. E., "Geronimo, the Apache Chief," *The Adobe Corral of the Westerners*, Tucson, Arizona, 1985.

Forbes, Donna, *L. A. Huffman: Pioneer Photographer*, Yellowstone Art Center, Billings, Montana, 1990.

Fowler, Don D., *The Western Photographs of John K. Hiller: Myself in the Water*, Smithsonian Institution Press, Washington and London, 1989.

Frederick Monsen at Hopi, foreword by Richard Rudisill, New Mexico Museum, Isleta Pueblo, New Mexico, 1979.

Frink, Maurice and Casey Barthelmess, *Photographer on an Army Mule*, University of Oklahoma Press, Norman, Oklahoma, 1965.

Gidley, M., *With One Sky Above Us*, G. P. Putnam & Sons, New York, 1979.

Goetzman, William H., *The First Americans*, Starwood Publishing, Washington, D.C., 1991.

Grabill, John, *Photographs of the Last Conflict Between the Sioux and the United States Military (1890-1891)*, South Dakota Historical Society.

Gray, John S., "Itinerant Frontier Photographers," *Montana Magazine of History*, Vol. 28, No. 2, Helena, Montana, 1978.

Index to the American Photographic Collections, George Eastman House, comp., G. K. Hall & Company, Boston, 1990.

Hamilton, Henry and Jean, *The Sioux of the Rosebud*, University of Oklahoma Press, Norman, Oklahoma, 1971.

Harrison, E. S., *Nome and Seward Peninsula*, Souvenir Edition, The Metropolitan Press, Seattle, 1905.

Hedren, Paul L., *With Crook in the Black Hills*, Pruett Publishing, Boulder, Colorado, 1985.

Heski, Thomas M., *The Little Shadow Catcher: D. F. Barry*, Superior Publishing, Seattle, 1978.

Hooper, Bruce, *Conservation News*.

Horan, J. D., and Paul Sann, *Pictorial History of the Wild West*, Crown Publishers Inc., New York, 1954.

Hough, Henry W., "Richard Throssel: Photographer of the Crows," *Denver Westerners Round Up*, Vol. 105, 1954.

Houlihan, Patrick T. and Betsy E., *Lummis in the Pueblos*, Northland Press, Flagstaff, Arizona, 1986.

Jensen, Paul, and John E. Carter, *Eyewitness at Wounded Knee*, University of Nebraska Press, Lincoln and London, 1991.

Johnston, Patricia Condon, "The Indian Photographs of Roland Reed," *The American West*, Montana, 1978.

Karson, Terry, Yellowstone Art Center, 1990.

Keegan, M. K., *Frontier Photographers, Enduring Culture, A Century of Photography of the Southwest Indians*, Clear Light Publishing, Santa Fe.

Lass, William E., "Eye to Eye," *Bulletin of the Graphic History Society of America*, Stanley J. Morrow, 1956.

Larson, *History of Montana*, Missoula County, Montana.

Mahood, Ruth I., *Photographer of the Southwest, Adam C. Vroman (1856-1916)*, The Ward Ritchie Press, Los Angeles, 1961.

Mangan, Terry, *Colorado on Glass*, Sundance Books, Denver, 1975.

Mattison, David, *Camera Workers, Camera Worker Press*, Vancouver City Archives, British Columbia, 1986.

Maurer, Stephen G., "Frederick Hamer Maude: Photographer of the Southwest," *Masterkey*, Southwest Museum, Los Angeles, California, 1985.

Moorhouse, Lee, *Souvenir Album of Noted Indian Photographs*, East Oregonian Printers, Pendleton, 1906.

Montana Directory, 1879.

Oregon Historical Quarterly, Vol. 49, 1948.

O'Connor, Nancy Fields and Fred Miller, *Photographer of the Crows*, University of Montana, Caravan Vidfilm, Inc., 1985.

Packard, Gar and Maggy, *Southwest 1880 with Ben Wittick, Pioneer Photographer*, Packard Publications, Santa Fe, New Mexico, 1970.

Palmquist, Peter, *With Nature's Children*, Interface California Corporation, Eureka, California, 1976.

Pearce-Moses, Richard, comp., *Photographic Collections in Texas*, Texas Historical Foundation, College Station, Texas, 1987.

Penot, Barbara Hale, "W. S. Prettyman," *Golden West*.

The Photographs of Frank B. Fiske, North Dakota Heritage Foundation, Inc., Bismarck, North Dakota.

Photographer's Encyclopedia International, 1839 to the Present, two vols.

Pinney, Patricia, *Dawes Centennial History*, Curtis Media Corp, Dallas.

Polk's Portland City Directory.

Prather, J. B., *Gold Fields of the Klondike: Photographs by Case & Draper*.

Rinehart, *Rinehart's Prints of American Indians*, Omaha, 1900.

Roberts, David L., *Wyoming Photographers of the Past*.

Rudisill, Richard, *Photographers of the New Mexico Territory (1854-1912)*, Musuem of New Mexico, Santa Fe, 1973.

Scherer, Joan C., *Indians*, Bonanza Books, New York, 1982.

Traywick, Ben T., *Camillus Sidney Fly: The Man Who Photographed History*, Red Marie's, 1985.

Wadsworth, Nelson B., *Through Camera Eyes*, Brigham Young University Press, 1975.

Watson, Elmo Scott, *Orlando Scott Goff: Pioneer Dakota Photographer*, 1962.

Webb, William, and R. A. Weinstein, *Dwellers at the Source*, University of New Mexico Press, Albuquerque, 1973.

Winslow, Mr. and Mrs., *A Pioneer Photographer, C. S. Baker*.

NEWSPAPERS:

Albuquerque Tribune, 1960

Arizona Daily Star, October 31, 1885

Chadron Journal, 1904, 1917, 1921, Dawes County, Nebraska

Denver Post, March 26, 1915, January 14, 1931

Ely Daily News, Nevada, 1972

Evening Herald, 1909

Fairfax Chief, February 26, 1931, Fairfax, Oklahoma

Kansas City Star, 1940

Rocky Mountain News, October 29, 1884, March 20, 1910, Denver

Sheridan Post Enterprise, August 25, 1927, Sheridan, Wyoming

INSTITUTIONS AND COLLECTIONS:

Canadian County Genealogical Society, El Reno, Oklahoma

Cherokee Strip Land Rush Museum, Perry, Oklahoma

Colorado Historical Society, Denver

Colorado College Library, Colorado Springs

Pike's Peak Library, Colorado Springs

Pioneer Museum, Colorado Springs

Addison, George Anthony 1, 2, 81
Alamosa 81
Alaska 20, 82
Alhambra 86
Alligator Joe 31
American Ethnology Department 83
American Horse 52, 86
Arapahoe 73, 74, 81, 88
Arco family 76
Arizona 81, 82, 84–86, 88, 89
Arkansas 82, 86
Arkansas City 86
Arrowrock Dam 85
Ashland County 87
Bailey, Dix & Meade 82
Bald Mountains 82
Barnum & Bailey Circus 83
Bartlesville 83
Beehive Geyser 82
Bellingham 83
Betsy Boston 67
Big Head 87
Bismarck 87
Black Dog 85
Black Hills 82, 85, 89
Black Tongue 16
Blackfoot 9
Blackwell 86
Bogardus, Abraham 3, 81
Bolivar 83
Bonaparte, Lucien 81
Bonaparte, Roland 4, 81
Bonine, Elia A. 5, 81
Boos, Edward Hugo 6, 81
Boston, Jacob Adam 7, 8, 81
Boulder Dam 85,
Bozeman Territory 82
Brockton 83
Brule Dakota 83
Buckskin Charlie 36, 53, 86
Buffalo Bill 3, 84, 85
Bureau of Reclamation 85
Butte City 87
C. Judd & Root Wool 84
Calfee, Henry Bird 9, 81
California 5, 81–89, 94
Calletano 13
Cambria 85,
Camera Work 40
Canada 84
Carmel 88
Carpenter, Charles Henry iv, 10, 11, 81
Castle Rock 88
Cayuse 26
Cedarville 87
Chadron 84
Chamberlain, William Gunnison 11, 12
Chase, Dana B. 13, 14, 81
Cherokee Strip 83

Cheyenne 3, 16, 21, 27, 61, 77, 78, 88
Chicago 82
Chicago Exposition 82
Chief Brave Heart 43
Chief Buckskin Charlie 36, 86
Chief Charlot 81
Chief Ignacio 81
Chief Iron Tail 29
Chief Joseph 28, 83
Chief Knife 71
Chief Little Wound 24
Chief Richard Big Kettle 85
Chief Skookum Wallahu 88
Chiricahua 10, 63, 87
Civil War 86, 87
Cocopah 81
Colorado 81, 82, 84, 86, 89
Colorado Springs 82, 84, 86
Columbia 83, 85, 88
Columbia River 83, 88
Columbian Exposition 82
Comanche 1, 2, 66, 76, 81
Conklin Studio 88
Connecticut 84
Cree 88
Crested Butte 81
Crockwell, James H. 15, 81
Cross, William Richard 16, 17, 81
Crow viii, 8, 57–59, 83, 85, 86, 88
Curley 83
Curtis, Asahel 18, 82
Curtis, Edward 82
Custer 83, 89
Dakota 83, 85, 87, 89
Deadwood 85,
Denmark 84
Denver 82, 86, 89
Dexter 87
Dick Charlie 7
Dobbs, Beverly 19, 20, 83
Drake, Jeremiah B. 21, 83
Drum, Oscar 22, 83
Durango 81, 86
Eason, Charles Leon 23, 24, 83
Eason, Ed 83
Eason, Helen 83
Eason, Will 83
East 81, 84, 86
El Reno 88
Elite 84
Erickson 84
Eskimo 19
Eureka 85
Field Museum 82
Fire Hole River 82
Flathead 6, 81
Florida 84
Fort Keogh 83,
Fort Sill 81
Fort Yates 87

Fouch, John Hale 25, 83
French Academy of Science 81
French Canadian 88
Galesburg 83
Gentle Annie 45
George Eagle Nest 72
Germany 84
Geronimo 10, 63, 82, 87, 89
Gifford, Benjamin A. 26, 83
Gill, Delancey W. 27, 28, 83
Glasier, Frank Whitman 29, 83
Glen Mammoth Springs 82
God Man 23
Goggle sisters 74, 88
Gold Hill 85
Gos Hutes 51
Grangeville City, Idaho 84
Graves, Ray W. 30, 83
Graves, Fay 83
Griggs, Frank 83
Gros Ventre 25
Hand, John Frederick 31, 84
Hand, Olive 84
Hanson, John Ankar 32, 84
Hartford 84,
Hartwell, Francis A. 33, 34, 84
Havasupai 45
Heyn Brothers, George and Herman 35, 84
Heyn Photo Supply Company 84
Hollow Horn Bear 83
Hook, William Edward 36, 84
Hopi 60, 82, 84, 89
Horse, Samuel American 52, 86
Huntington 6, 85
Illinois 6, 83, 87
Indian 4, 9, 57, 69, 81–89
  artifacts 84, 85
  delegations 83
  dirge 85
  leaders 87
  police 69, 87
  wars 86
Indiana 87
Iowa 84
Isleta Pueblo 79, 89
Jack Red Cloud 87
Jake 13
James, George Wharton 37, 38, 84
Jicarilla 87
John Grass 87
Judd, Edwin Young 39, 84
Kansas 86, 87, 88
Kasebier, Gertrude 40, 85
Kentucky 81, 86
Kills the Enemy 87
Kiowa 81, 88
Lakota 86
Lamanda Park 5, 81
Lancaster 81

Lander 87, 88
Latham, Edward 41, 42, 85
Lawton City 81
Lead City 85
Lincoln 83
Little Bear 73
Little Eagle 86
Locke, Henry R. 43, 85
Lodge Grass 86
Lone Wolf 65
Los Angeles 85, 88, 89
Louisiana Purchase Exposition 82, 83
Lubken, Walter John 44, 85
Lumiere Studio 84
Mad Bear 87
Madonna 26
Maine 82,
Makah 18, 67
Manitou Springs 84
Maria 6
Maricopa 33, 34, 84
Massachusetts 83, 87
Maude, Frederick Hamer 45–48, 85
Mayodgap 75
Memaloose Island 88
Mescalero 87
Mexico 82–85, 86, 88, 89
Meyer, Fred R. 49, 85
Michigan 84
Mikinas 21,
Miniconju 86,
Minnesota 83, 84, 89,
Mississippi 81
Missoula 81
Missoula Mercantile Company 81
Missouri 6, 82, 83, 88
Mohave 81, 87
Moki 38
Monaco, Louis 50, 51, 85
Monaco, Luigi Natale 85
Montana 81, 82, 84–89
Monterey 88
Morledge, Clarence G. 52, 85
Mount Hood 83
Nast, Charles A. 53, 86
Navajo 11, 14, 37, 55, 56, 84
Nebraska 82–84, 87, 88
Nevada 82, 85
Nevada Gulch 82
New Haired Horse 30
New Mexico 82, 84–86, 88, 89
New York 81, 84–86, 89
Nez Perce 28, 32, 42
Niobrara 82
Nome 21, 89
North Carolina 81
Northwest 82, 87
Oglala Sioux 23, 24
Ohio 81, 86, 87
Oklahoma 81, 83, 86, 88, 89
Oklahoma City 83
Old Faithful Geyser 82
Omaha Dancers 85
Oraibi Pueblo 38, 47
Oregon 83, 84, 88
Oregon Camera Club 88

Osage 22, 54, 86
Pagosa Springs 81
Painted Horse 35
Pan Pacific Exposition 87
Paonia 81,
Paris, Missouri 88,
Parsons, George W. 55, 86
Pasadena 6, 81, 89
Paul Elk 87
Pawhuska 86
Pawnee Bill Show 86,
Pendleton Woolen Mills 84
Pennington, William Marion 55, 56, 86
Pennsylvania 81, 85–89
Petzoldt, William Augustus 57–59, 86
Philadelphia 85, 87
Phoebe Wilpatin 42
Pine Ridge Agency 85
Piute 50
Poley, Horace Swartley 60, 86
Ponca City 83
Portland 83
Prairie Chief 28
Pretty Voice 68, 87
Prettyman and Cornish 86
Prettyman, William 61, 86
Pueblo 14, 48, 79, 81, 89
Queen Mine 81
Randall, A. Frank 62, 87
Rau, William 63, 64, 87
Ray, Benjamin Franklin 65, 87
Red Cloud 23, 49, 87
Red Tomahawk 69, 70, 87
Redvale 81
Ringling Circus 83
Rochester, New York 86
Rodoker, David H. 66, 87
Rosebud Agency 82
Rushville 87
Rutter, THomas H. 67, 87
Saguache 81
Saint Francis School 82
Salem 88
Samuel American Horse 52, 86
San Carlos Reservation 87
San Francisco 84, 85, 89
San Ildefonso 8
San Juan 82
Santa Clara 15, 82
Santa Clara Pueblo 15
Santa Fe 82
Santa Fe Southern Railway 82
Scalp Dance 85
Scott, George W. 68–71, 87
Sells Circus
Seminole 31
Seneca 85
Shavano 11
She Came Spotted 86
Shoshone 75, 87
Shuck, Joseph A. 72, 73, 87
Sioux iv, 4, 17, 23, 24, 30, 35, 43, 82,
   87, 89
Sitting Bull 82
South Dakota 85, 89

Southwest 82, 85, 89
Southwest Museum 85
Spanish missions 85
Sparks Circus 83
Spearfish 85
Spokane 85
Sproul, Charles E. 74, 88
St. Louis 63, 74, 82–84, 87, 88
Stampede 30
Stimson, Joseph Elam 75, 88
Stotz, Christopher Charles 76, 77, 88
Switzerland 85,
Texas 81, 89
The Manager 84
The Red Man 40, 85
Throssel, Richard viii, 78, 88
Tommy Jumper 31
Towee 53
Trinidad 82
Union Pacific 87
United States 81, 89
University of Rochester 86
Utah 82
Ute 7, 8, 11, 12, 15, 36, 81, 86
Victorian 81
Virginia City 85
Waite, Charles B. 79, 88
Walapai 84
Wa-rets 11
Washington 81, 83, 87, 89
West 81, 83, 85, 88, 89
White Bull 87
White, Lily Edith 80, 88
White Mountain Apache 87
White Skunk 66
White Swan 4
Wholesale View Company 84
Wild West shows 83
William Prettyman 61, 86
Wind River Reservation 88
Winfield 87
Wolf Voice 25
Wounded Knee 86, 94
Wyoming 85, 87, 88
Yakima 44, 87
Yellow Horn 87
Yellow Shirt iv
Yellow Wolf 41
Yellowstone 82, 83, 88, 89
Yukon 82
Yuma 5, 81, 87
Zuni 84

A portion of the proceeds from this book will be donated by the compiler to the Wounded Knee sub-district Youth Center Activities.

Send all correspondences to the author at:
Edward McAndrew
7530 Fountain Ave. #10
Los Angeles, California
90046